SCIENCE DARES YOU!™

Build a
ROCKET BOAT

And 18 more
wild wind projects!

D0170153

by Sandra Markle

Illustrated by Eric Brace

SCHOLASTIC INC.

New York   Toronto   London   Auckland   Sydney
Mexico City   New Delhi   Hong Kong   Buenos Aires

For dear friends Wayne and Gail Rissman. —S.M.

For my favorite nephew, my only nephew...
the one with my exact same name.
Here's to Eric, not me, my nephew.—E.B.

The author would like to thank Dr. John Campbell, Department of Physics, University of Canterbury, Christchurch, New Zealand, for sharing his expertise and enthusiasm. As always, a special thanks to Skip Jeffery for his help and support.

ISBN 0-439-44433-0

Text copyright © 2003 by Sandra Markle.
Illustrations copyright © 2003 by Scholastic Inc.

12 11 10 9 8 7 6 5 4 3 2 1   3 4 5 6 7 8/0

Printed in the U.S.A.
First printing, March 2003
Design by Jennifer Rinaldi Windau

SCIENCE DARES YOU TO . . .

Note to Parents and Teachers: The books in the Science Dares You! series encourage children to wonder why and to investigate to find out. While they have fun exploring, young readers discover basic science concepts related to each book's theme. They also develop problem-solving strategies they can use when tackling any challenge.

In *Science Dares You! Build a Rocket Boat*, children tackle challenges that help them become empowered to ask questions and seek solutions. In the process, they develop an understanding of one of Earth's materials, air, by investigating its properties and the force moving air can exert. "Scientists use different kinds of investigations depending on the questions they are trying to answer. Types of investigations include describing objects, events, and organisms; classifying them, and doing a fair test (experimenting)." (National Science Education Standards, as identified by the National Academy of Sciences)

SCIENCE DARES YOU TO
GET BLOWN AWAY!

WHAT IF you could lift a book without touching it, inflate a balloon without blowing into it, or build a rocket boat that *speeds across the water* without an engine? Believe it or not, you can do all of these things—*and lots more*—when you tackle the dares in this book. All you need is some creativity, a little help from Science, and an **amazing**, **easy-to-find** substance:

AIR.

The Basics

First, you need to know something about air. Even though you can't see it, air takes up space and can be squeezed together. Air is made up of tiny particles called *molecules*. Because it is made up of molecules, air also has weight. The weight of air pressing against something is called *air pressure*. The more air molecules are packed tightly together, the greater the air pressure. When air is cooled, the molecules move closer together. But when air is heated, the molecules move farther apart. So warm air has less air pressure than cool air.

Like water, air flows. It moves from an area of higher air pressure to an area of lower pressure. Moving air is called *wind*, and wind has force. The faster the air flows, the stronger the wind. Powerful winds, like tornadoes and hurricanes, have enough force to damage buildings and uproot trees. So you may be surprised to discover one more thing about air: fast-moving air has less air pressure than slow-moving air. This may seem hard to believe, but in some of the dares in this book, you'll prove it to yourself!

STAY SAFE!

✘ Always check with an adult partner to be sure the way you plan to meet each dare will be safe for you to try.
✘ Never, ever put anything you are testing into your mouth unless you know it's safe to do so.

You're almost ready to get blown away as you put air to work! But first, here are some tips that will help you meet each science challenge.

HELPFUL HINTS

 Brainstorm ways to tackle the challenge. Use the clues provided to help you think of possibilities. Then list three to five things you could try.

 Choose which ideas would be most likely to work. Don't forget to check with an adult to be sure your idea is safe for you to test.

 Test your idea, and see what happens. Did you meet the dare?

Once you've thought about the dare, you can follow the instructions to try out one strategy that will work.

Now you're ready to get blown away. Good luck—and don't forget to have fun!

BUILD A ROCKET BOAT

Your challenge is to make a boat that's
powered by a blast of air. Can you do it?
Check out the clues, then start inventing!

Clues

✗ Blow up a balloon but don't seal the neck. Then hold the
balloon over your head and let go. What happens? How
could this help you meet the dare?

✗ What could you use to control the direction air is released
from a balloon? Which of these items would be cheap and
safe to test?

Take the Dare!

You'll need:

> **Adult partner**
> **Scissors with pointed ends**
> **Quart-sized plastic milk jug with a screw-on cap**
> **Rubber balloon**
> **Twist tie**
> **Bathtub or outdoor wading pool**

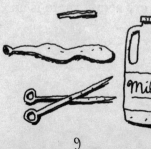

1. Have your adult partner use the pointed scissors to poke a hole through the milk jug cap. The hole should be big enough to thread the balloon's neck through easily.

2. Have him or her also put a small hole on the front of the milk jug above the label.

3. Thread the balloon's neck through the milk jug cap hole. Put the balloon inside the milk jug and screw on the cap.

4. Blow up the balloon, twist the neck outside the cap, and seal with the twist tie.

5. To launch your rocket ship, place the jug in the water, label side up, and untwist the tie. The ship should zoom ahead. If it doesn't, wait until the balloon deflates. Then, have your adult partner enlarge the hole in the jug lid slightly so the air can escape faster. Test it again.

What Happened?

The balloon released a rush of air in one direction—backward—and this moved the boat in the opposite direction—forward. This is a basic law of motion: For every action there is an equal and opposite reaction.

SHOOT A BALLOON
AT A TARGET

To meet this dare, you'll need to invent
a way to control a balloon's flight path so it
travels along a string. So start brainstorming!

Clues

✘ Make a list of all the things you could use to attach a balloon to a string. Which of these would let the balloon move
along the string?

✘ Examine a plastic straw. Could this straw help you control
the balloon's flight path?

Take the Dare!

You'll need:

10-foot-long (3-meter-) piece of string
Plastic straw
Table leg
Chair with a back
Rubber balloon
Twist tie
Masking tape

1. Thread the 10-foot- (3-meter-) long piece of string
through a straw. Stretch the string from a table leg to the top
of a chair back. Tie both ends.

12

2. Slide the straw to one end of the string.

3. Inflate the balloon and use the twist tie to seal the neck.

4. Tape the balloon to the straw. Position the balloon so the nose is aimed toward the other end of the string.

5. Undo the twist tie. Your balloon should speed toward the target.

6. If the balloon doesn't go far enough to reach the target, try taping a second balloon below or beside the first. Have a partner help you release both balloons at the same time.

What Happened?

When air shot out of the balloon in one direction, the balloon moved in the opposite direction. The straw held the balloon to the string and kept it on course.

WOW! A sneeze is a fast wind blasting out of your body. In fact, during a sneeze, scientists have recorded particles being propelled out of the mouth and nose as fast as 100 miles (160 kilometers) per hour!

A
Historic
Dare

When the valuable Solar Max
satellite needed repairs in the early
1980s, NASA engineers had to figure
out a way for an astronaut to fix it.
An astronaut would need to leave
the space shuttle, fly through space,
and return to the ship. So NASA
scientists invented the MMU
(Manned Maneuvering Unit),
a backpack with twenty-four
nitrogen gas jets. Using little blasts
of gas to propel himself and to steer,
astronaut George "Pinky" Nelson
successfully repaired the
satellite and returned safely
to the shuttle.

LIFT A BOOK WITH ONLY YOUR BREATH

This dare may sound pretty tough to tackle, but
don't worry. You can meet it with a little help from science.

Clues

✗ Hold your hand about two inches (5 centimeters) from your
face and breathe out as you normally would. You'll feel
your breath. What could you do to make your breath come
out in a more powerful gust?

✗ Compare a balloon that's not inflated
with one that's blown up. How did
filling the balloon with air change it?
How could that change help you
meet the dare?

Take the Dare!

You'll need:

Rubber balloon
Table
24- to 40-page book

1. Place the balloon on the table so the neck extends over the edge.

2. Set the book on the balloon. Be careful not to cover the neck of the balloon. Blow into the balloon.

3. Watch the balloon rise in the air. You've met the dare!

What Happened?

Your breath is air. When you blow out through your mouth, you force out as much air as you can. You also direct the air where you want it to go. Blowing into the balloon pushed the balloon outward in all directions. The balloon inflated, and that lifted the book.

DOUBLE DARE #1

Science dares you to find a way to use air to support your weight. Have you ever used air to keep yourself afloat? Or, have you ever slept on a cushion of air? If so, those experiences will help you solve this Double Dare.

BUILD A WATER CANNON

How can you turn a squirt bottle into
a cannon that blasts out water?
Let science give you a hand.

Clues

✗ Build this squirt bottle to use when you test your ideas.
Have an adult partner use sharp scissors to make a hole
about 2 inches (5 centimeters) above the base of an empty
two-liter plastic soft-drink bottle. Cover the hole with tape
and fill the bottle with water. Set the bottle on the edge of
the sink with the hole facing the drain. To see the bottle
squirt, uncover the hole. The force of the air pressing down
on the water makes the water squirt out. This force is
called air pressure. Could increasing the air pressure help
you to meet this dare?

✗ Look around the house for things you could use to store air
and release it all at once into the bottle. How could that
help you meet this dare?

WOW! Squirt guns used to just shoot out a stream of water, and early models could shoot water only about 8 feet (about 3 meters). Then, in 1982, U.S. aerospace engineer Lonnie Johnson had an idea. With the help of inventor Bruce D'Andrade, Johnson created a pump-action squirt gun that used air pressure to blast water. Johnson's new squirt gun could shoot water as far as 50 feet (about 15 meters)!

Take the Dare!

You'll need:

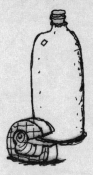

Rubber balloon
Twist tie
Tape
The squirt bottle you made (see Clues, page 18)
Bathroom or kitchen sink
Adult partner

1. Inflate the balloon, twist the neck shut, and hold it while your adult partner seals it with a twist tie. Leave as much of the neck of the balloon free below the twist tie, toward the mouth of the balloon, as possible.

2. Put tape over the hole in your squirt bottle and fill it up.

3. Set the bottle on the edge of the sink, with the hole aimed toward the drain.

4. Slide the mouth of the balloon over the top of the bottle, and hold it so the balloon stays on.

5. Have your adult partner pull the tape off the squirt bottle. You should undo the twist tie at the same time. The water should shoot out of the squirt bottle. Congratulations—you've met the dare!

What Happened?

Once the air inside the balloon had a way to escape, it rushed out into the bottle. This increased the air pressure pushing on the water. And that forced the water out through the hole. The stronger the air pressure, the more powerful the water blast.

DOUBLE WOW!

• Today, fire trucks can pump 750 gallons (2840 liters) of water per minute. The pressure of that much water shooting through a hose can make the hose hard to handle. Usually several people are needed to direct the spray of water at the fire.

DOUBLE DARE #2

Does exercising make you increase or decrease how much air you take in with each breath? Science dares you to design an experiment using the water cannon to find out.

USE AIR TO TRAP WINE WATER IN A GLASS

Can you hold a glass full of water
upside down without spilling a drop?
You can if you meet this dare!

Clues

✗ The air around you pushes in every direction on every surface it touches. How might this help you meet this dare?

✗ Air has weight. To see that for yourself, tie an 8-inch-long
piece of string to an inflated balloon. Tie another string to
a balloon that's not inflated. Tape one string to each end of
a yardstick or a meter stick. Next, tie a string to the center
of the stick and hold it so the balloons are off the floor. The
air-filled balloon will hang down farther than the empty
balloon because it's heavier.

Take the Dare!

You'll need:

A small glass
Water
Paper towel
Sturdy plastic picnic plate

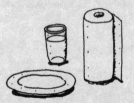

*Note: This dare can make a mess, so check with an adult to
see where you should experiment.*

23

1. Fill the glass nearly full of water.

2. Fold the paper towel into fourths and place it on the middle of the plate.

3. Place the plate, towel side down, over the glass.

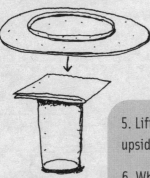

4. Hold the glass with one hand and put the other hand on the center of the plate to hold it against the glass.

5. Lift and turn the glass and plate upside down.

6. When the glass is straight, remove the hand holding the plate. You've met the dare because the water stays suspended inside the glass.

What Happened?

The air pressure outside the glass, pushing up, was greater than the pressure of the air and water inside the glass, pushing down. It was strong enough to trap the water. Be sure to hold the glass straight at all times, though. If you tip the glass, air can slip inside, spoiling that pressure balance. Then you not only won't meet the dare, you'll get wet!

MAKE AN AIR BUBBLE
DIVE UNDERWATER

Can you make an air bubble rise or sink
when you want to? Check out the clues to start
brainstorming how to meet this dare.

Clues

✘ Fill a clear plastic bottle three-quarters full of water and
screw on the lid. Gently squeeze the sides of the bottle and
watch the amount of air above the water shrink. The air is
being *compressed*, or squeezed. How could being able to
compress air in a bottle help you meet this dare?

✘ Collect several foil packets of ketchup, soy sauce, or salad
dressing. Squeeze gently to feel the air bubble trapped
inside. How could a trapped air bubble help you meet this
dare?

Take the Dare!

You'll need:

Glass full of water
Several foil packets of ketchup, soy sauce,
    or salad dressing
Clear, empty 2-liter plastic bottle with a screw-on lid

1. Fill the glass with water and drop in the foil packets to see which floats best. Make that one your test packet.

2. Fill the bottle almost full of water.

3. Gently push in the test packet.

4. Add more water so the bottle is as full as it can be.

5. Screw on the lid.

6. Squeeze the sides of the bottle to make the packet sink. When you stop squeezing, the packet will rise again. Congratulations—you've met the dare!

What Happened?

An object floats when the amount of water the object pushes aside can support its weight. When you squeezed the bottle you increased the pressure inside the bottle. That squeezed the air bubble inside the packet. The air bubble became smaller, slightly changing how much water the packet pushed aside. That meant the packet didn't float quite as well, and it sank a little. When you stopped squeezing the bottle, the pressure decreased. Then the air bubble expanded again and the packet rose inside the bottle.

DOUBLE DARE #3

Science dares you to come up with something you could use in place of the foil packet to trap an air bubble underwater.

WOW! Many fish have a gas-filled sac, called the swim bladder, to help them dive and float up in the water. But for many fish the swim bladder does something more—it helps them produce sounds. By making muscles surrounding the swim bladder squeeze and relax, the fish makes its swim bladder vibrate. That produces sounds like grunts, groans, thuds, and even barks. Some fish also have a connection between their inner ear and their swim bladder. In these fish, the swim bladder doesn't just help them make sounds—it also helps them hear. That can be very important when a fish is trying to find a mate somewhere in that great big sea.

DOUBLE WOW!

A submarine dives by letting water into air-filled tanks called ballast tanks. As this pushes the air out escape vents, the ship sinks. To surface, compressed air forces the water out again. A submarine can shoot up to the surface from the ocean depths in a matter of seconds. It uses a supply of high-pressure air to push out hundreds of tons of stored water.

BLOW OUT A CANDLE THROUGH A GLASS JAR

Sound impossible? It's not!

Take the Dare!

You'll need:

Candle stub (no bigger than half of a full-sized candle)
Short candleholder
Cookie sheet
Quart jar
Blow dryer
Matches
Adult partner

1. Ask your adult partner to help you choose a safe place to conduct this test.

2. Place the candle in the holder, making sure it fits snugly, and set the candle on the cookie sheet.

3. Place the glass jar in front of the candleholder, close enough to almost touch the holder.

4. Make sure the top of the jar is a little higher than the top of the candle. If necessary, elevate the jar.

5. Plug in the blow dryer.

6. To perform the test, have your adult partner light the candle.

7. Aim the blow dryer at the middle of the glass jar and switch it on "high." The candle should flicker and go out.

What Happened?

The blast of air from the blow dryer struck the glass jar and flowed around its curved surface. When the air reached the candle, it blew out the flame.

A Historic Dare

IN THE 1970S, scientists figured out a new use for an old tool: the windmill. The air spun the windmill around, and that motion provided power to operate machinery. Windmills can even power a generator to make electricity. These are called wind turbines. The world's largest group of wind turbines is near San Francisco, California. It contains 6,000 wind turbines.

FLOAT A PING-PONG BALL IN MIDAIR

It will look like you're performing magic
when you meet this dare.

Clues

✗ How much do you know about fast-moving air? Cut a 2-inch- (5-centimeter-) wide strip from a sheet of notebook paper. Next, use both hands to hold the top edge of the paper just below your lips, so that the paper is hanging vertically. Then, take a deep breath and blow down on the paper. Surprise! Instead of being pushed down by this blast of fast-moving air, the paper lifts. That's because flowing air has less pressure than stationary air.

✗ Look at a funnel. How could you use this tool to surround a Ping-Pong ball with your breath?

Take the Dare!

You'll need:

Plastic or metal funnel just big enough for the ball to fit inside the cone
Ping-Pong ball

1. Turn the funnel so the large cone is pointed down.

2. Hold the Ping-Pong ball inside the funnel, put your mouth over the small end of the funnel, and blow out hard.

3. Let go of the ball while you blow. The ball should stay in place as long as you keep on blowing. If it drops, you need to blow harder. Or have your adult partner take a deep breath and blow for you.

What Happened?

The fast-moving air inside the funnel had less air pressure than the air outside the funnel. The harder you blew, the faster the flow of air and the lower the air pressure inside the funnel's cone. As long as you kept blowing, the ball was supported by higher-pressure air outside the funnel.

WOW!

If you want to experience some really strong winds, visit Mount Washington in New Hampshire. On April 12, 1934, weather instruments on that mountain's top measured the wind speed at 188 miles per hour (about 303 kilometers per hour) with gusts up to 231 miles per hour (372 kilometers per hour). That's still the world's wind speed record, but even on a good day Mount Washington is very windy. On average, hurricane-force winds are recorded there several times a week.

DOUBLE DARE #4

Science dares you to figure out a way to use a blow dryer to make a Ping-Pong ball float in midair.

MAKE A KITE—THEN FLY IT

Get creative! But before you start
designing, check out the clues
to get some helpful tips.

Clues

✘ Remember, fast-moving air has less air pressure than
slow-moving air. Think of ways you might be able to make
air flow faster over the top surface of a kite. How might
this help you meet the dare?

✘ Look at photos of airplane wings. You'll discover that the
upper surface is usually curved while the lower surface is
flat. How might modeling your kite after this shape help
you meet this dare?

Take the Dare!

You'll need:

> Scissors
> Large (leaf bag size) plastic trash bag—it's best if
>   it's not black
> Red permanent marker
> Ruler
> Transparent tape
> Hole punch
> 3 wooden dowels, 36 inches (90 centimeters) long
>   by $1/8$ inch (1.6 centimeters) in diameter

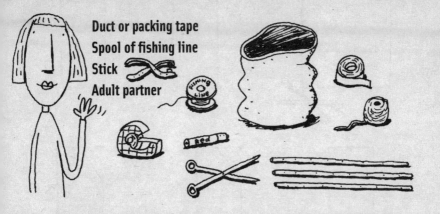

Duct or packing tape
Spool of fishing line
Stick
Adult partner

1. Cut the trash bag open to form a large plastic sheet. Cut a 36-inch (90-centimeter) square out of the plastic sheet.

2. Fold the plastic in half.

3. Measure 10 inches (25 centimeters) to the left of the fold, along the top edge of the sheet. Use the marker to mark that point. Label this mark "A."

4. Measure 12 inches (30 centimeters) down from the left top corner and make a mark. Label this mark "B."

5. Draw a line between these two marks and cut off the left corner.

6. Measure 10 inches (25 centimeters) to the left of the fold along the bottom edge of the sheet. Make a mark and label it "C." Draw a line between "B" and "C" and cut off the left bottom corner.

7. Unfold the sheet.

1.)

2.)

3.)

4.) A
B

5.) A
B

6.) A
B
C

7.)

8.)

9.)

10.)

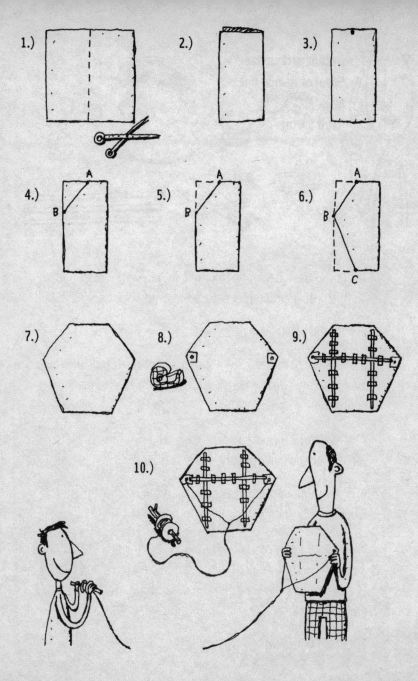

8. Reinforce the two corners of the plastic with transparent tape. Then, make a hole through the tape and plastic with the hole punch.

9. Lay the wooden dowels on the plastic—one at the center, and one at each mark to the left and right. Be sure the dowels are straight and anchor with the tape.

10. Cut a piece of fishing line about 70 inches (175 centimeters) long and tie it to the two holes.

11. Tie the free end of the remaining spool of fishing line to the center of this line. Now the kite is ready to fly. A stick poked through the spool of fishing line will let you feed the line out more easily.

12. To launch your kite, stand with your back to the wind while your partner walks away holding the top of the kite pointed straight up.

13. When you're about 20 feet (6 meters) apart, signal for your partner to release the kite as you pull in on the line. This will slant the kite so its face is held at an angle to the wind. If the kite doesn't climb, repeat this process.

14. Once your kite is airborne, pull in on the line a little. When you feel the kite tug, feed out a little line until it goes slack. Then, repeat the process.

What Happened?

The kite flew because the air pressure was greater under the kite than over it. That created *lift*.

How fast the wind is blowing will affect how well your kite flies. The ideal wind speed is between five and fifteen miles (eight to twenty-four kilometers) per hour. If you aren't sure if the wind speed is right for kite flying, check for some natural signs. You should see leaves moving, dust blowing, or flags lifting. But if trees are swaying or flags are flapping, the wind is probably too strong. Remember, never run to launch your kite, because you could fall. Be sure to fly your kite in an open area clear of any power lines or trees.

DOUBLE DARE #5

Science dares you to design an experiment to test how adding a tail affects a kite's flight.

A Historic Dare

IN THE 1820s, carriages in England were charged a road toll, depending on the number of horses powering the carriage. So George Pocock figured out a way to travel for free by replacing his two horses with two kites. His lightweight carriage was able to carry up to five passengers at speeds as fast as twenty miles (32 kilometers) per hour, depending on the wind speed. Of course, on a calm day, Pocock had to stay home.

INFLATE A BALLOON WITH AN EMPTY SODA BOTTLE

Does it sound like you'll need magic
to meet this dare? You don't—the clues will point you
in the right direction.

Clues

✗ Even though an empty bottle looks empty, it's really full of
air. How can you get the air from the bottle into a balloon?

✗ If you've ever seen steam over boiling water, you've seen
what happens to heated air. It rises. How could heat help
you meet this dare?

Take the Dare!

You'll need:

Rubber balloon
Sink with running hot water
Bowl
1-liter empty plastic water or soft-drink bottle
Adult partner

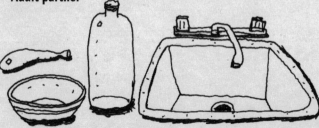

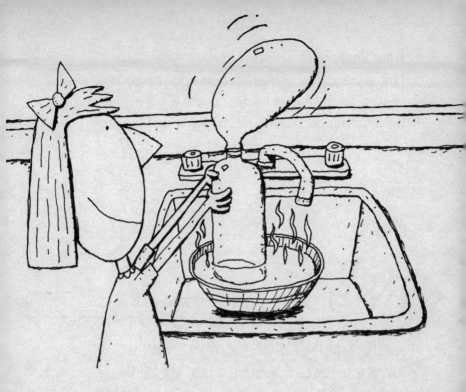

1. Place the neck of the balloon over the mouth of the bottle.

2. Run water in the sink until it's hot. Ask an adult for help so you don't burn yourself.

3. Set the bowl in the sink and fill it about half full of water.

4. Lay the bottle on the hot water. Almost instantly, the balloon will inflate. Even though it won't inflate as much as if you'd blown into it, you've met the dare.

What Happened?

Hot air rises. So when the air inside the bottle heated up, it rose as far as it could go. Then it became trapped inside the balloon, making it inflate.

WOW! The sun's energy heats up some parts of the Earth's surface more than others. On September 13, 1922, the record temperature ever recorded on Earth was 138°F (about 58°C) at Al Aziziya, Libya, in Africa. And that temperature was recorded in the shade! Death Valley, California, in the United States is also a very hot spot. The hottest temperature ever recorded there was 134°F (about 57°C).

A Historic Dare

In 1783, more than a hundred years before the Wright Brothers launched the first airplane, two other brothers discovered a different way to fly. Frenchmen Jacques and Joseph Montgolfier designed a hot air balloon. Before sending people up, they tested their invention with three animals: a duck, a rooster, and a sheep. When that worked, they tried human passengers. Marquis d'Arlandes and Pilatre de Rosier became the first humans to fly. They soared upward riding in a basket dangling beneath a large, smoke-filled cloth bag.

UNCOVER A BURIED TREASURE WITHOUT DIGGING

You have a bag of quarters buried in a pile of dirt,
but you can't dig it out. How can you reach the loot?

Clues

✘ You have probably seen dirt blowing down the street or across a bare field. How could wind help you meet this dare?

✘ List all of the things you can find around the house that can move air, producing wind. How might one of these help you meet this dare?

Take the Dare!

You'll need:

7 quarters
Small plastic resealable bag
1 cup of flour
Adult partner
Straw

NOTE: *You're going to make a mess, so check with your adult partner to see where you should experiment.*

1. Put all the quarters in the bag.

2. Set the bag of quarters on your work area and cover the bag with a pile of flour.

3. Be sure any observers are behind you.

4. Aim the straw at the flour and blow hard.

What Happened?

Your breath had enough force to move the flour. The harder you blew, the stronger the blast of air became.

☞ A Historic Dare ☜

During World War I, wind started blowing away the topsoil on farms, and farmers had an important dare to meet—how to stop this from happening. The farmers had cleared millions of acres of grasslands, hoping to make big profits by growing wheat. Unfortunately, the wheat plants didn't anchor the soil as well as the buffalo grass and other natural vegetation. Long periods without rain made the situation worse. Wind erosion, or wind carrying away soil, created dust clouds so thick people called them "black blizzards." Finally, farmers met nature's challenge by replanting millions of acres of native grasses to anchor the soil between fields of grain. They also planted rows of trees to act as windbreaks. Over time, these efforts helped restore the land. Then, rising wheat prices encouraged them to plow up the grasslands again. Finally, the U.S. government helped farmers balance their need to earn money with their need to prevent wind erosion. The Soil Bank Program was established to pay farmers to keep part of their land planted in grass.

MAKE MUSIC
WITH A STRAW

You know you can blow air through
a straw, but how can you use your breath
to make music? Read the clues to help you start brainstorming.

Clues

✗ Anything that *vibrates*, or moves back and forth in the
same path again and again, can create waves in the air.
Your ears detect these and your brain interprets them as
sounds. What can you do to a straw to make it vibrate?

✗ Pour water into two identical glasses. Fill one half full and
the other almost as full as it can be. Tap the side of each
glass with a metal spoon. The half-full glass makes a lower
sound. That's because the taller the column of vibrating air,
the lower the sound. How can you change the amount of air
vibrating inside a straw?

Take the Dare!

You'll need:

Scissors
5 plastic straws
Adult partner

1. Cut the end of each straw into a V-shaped point. Flatten the "V" with your thumbnail. Then, use one of the following two strategies to vary the length of the air columns inside the straws:

- Cut the straws so they are five different lengths.

- Have an adult partner use a sharp scissor tip or knife point to poke three holes in one straw. Place one hole in the center of the straw's length. Place the other two holes at equal distances on either side of the first hole.

2. To create a sound with the straw, put the "V" between your lips and blow.

3. If you cut the straws, blow through each one in turn, listening to the sounds. If you cut holes in the straw, cover the holes with your fingers and blow. Then repeat, blowing as you lift different fingers to uncover the holes one at a time, two at a time, or all at once.

4. You can use your straws to play a song, "Mary Had a Little Lamb," by following the pattern below. The highest sounding note is number 1 and the lowest sounding note is number 3.

1, 2, 3, 2, 1, 1, 1

2, 2, 2,1, 1, 1

1, 2, 3, 2, 1, 1, 1

1, 2, 2, 1, 2, 3

Now, create and play a tune of your own!

What Happened?

When you blew through the "V," the force of this moving air made the plastic straw vibrate. And that created airwaves inside the straw. The length of this column of air depended on the straw's length. Or it depended on the length of the column of air before it reached a hole. The longer the column of moving air was, the lower the sound.

TURN APPLESAUCE
INTO APPLE LEATHER

You won't believe how easy it is to use
air to make this old-time candy.

Clues

✘ After a bath, your towel is damp, but by the next day it's
dry. What happens to the water? How might this drying
process help you meet the dare?

✘ Cut up an apple and place one slice on a pie plate. Have an
adult partner place the pie plate in an oven and heat at
200°F (about 90°C) for five minutes. How could heat help
you meet this dare?

Take the Dare!

You'll need:

1 cup of applesauce
Cake pan
Cinnamon (optional)
Oven
Adult partner
Fork
Oven mitt
Cooling rack
Powdered suga

1. Pour the applesauce into the center of the cake pan. If you want to add cinnamon, sprinkle on a pinch and stir to mix.

2. Spread out the sauce to form a thin even layer.

3. Bake at 200°F (about 90°C) for an hour or until your adult partner pokes the sauce with a fork and finds it's leathery.

4. Have your adult partner use the oven mitt to move the pan to the cooling rack and sprinkle the apple leather with powdered sugar.

5. You've met the dare. So once the pan is cool, peel out the apple leather and pull off pieces to munch.

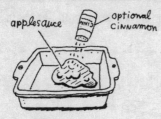

applesauce optional cinnamon

Step 1.

Step 2.

THIN eVeN Layer

Bake at 200°F for about an hour.

Step 3.

Remove pan from oven, let cool, and sprinkle with powdered sugar.

Step 4.

What Happened?

The applesauce lost much of its moisture. You could have dried the applesauce the way the pioneers used to by just letting it sit. Air moving across the surface of the sauce caused the water to slowly *evaporate* or move into the air. Heating the applesauce in the oven sped up this process. Not only is apple leather tasty, it won't mold quickly the way applesauce will. In fact, one of the ways people used to preserve food for use during the winter was to dry it.

WOW!

In just one growing season, a single corn plant may give off as much as 44 gallons (200 liters) of water. Green plants have tiny openings in their leaves through which water flows out—just the way you sweat. Then, the water evaporates, moving into the air.

A Historic Dare

WHEN **NASA** FIRST sent people into space
for days and even weeks, they needed a
way to send plenty of food with them.
This food needed to be lightweight, because
the more a spacecraft weighed the more
fuel it needed. So researchers developed
freeze-dried foods. During the flight,
astronauts prepared the food by adding water.
It was the perfect space-food solution!

WOW!

Thunder is nature's big sound.
This deep rumbling is created when a lightning bolt
quickly heats up the air. The sudden heat creates an explosive
airwave. Amazingly, lightning and thunder happen somewhere
on Earth more than a hundred times every second!

DOUBLE DARE #6

Science dares you to stop a leaf
from giving off water.

The annual average at Yuma, Arizona, USA, is 91% of the possible hours of sunshine (a mean of 4055 hours out of 4456 possible hours in a year). St. Petersburg, in Florida, USA, recorded 768 consecutive sunny days from February 9, 1967, to March 17, 1969.

Scientists estimate that an amount of air as big as a sugar cube contains billions of air molecules. And those molecules are constantly on the move, bumping into each other.

If it were possible to use the air blowing in a hurricane to produce electricity, scientists estimate one of these storms could power up the whole United States for three years.

Scientists have found a way to collect samples of air from the Earth's ancient past. This air is trapped as tiny bubbles inside the ice sheets covering much of Antarctica.

If the Earth were no bigger than an apple, all of the air surrounding the Earth would be about as thick as the apple's peel.

Every day, you breathe in about 130 times your body volume in air.

#1 Your bicycle tires contain compressed air. So when you ride your bike, compressed air is supporting your weight. If you've ever rested on an inflated air mattress, you've also been supported by compressed air.

#2 Remember to keep all of the conditions the same except whether or not you've exercised before blowing into the bottle. And repeat each test at least three times to make sure the results are what's likely to happen every time.

   Before you blow into the squirt bottle, take three deep breaths. Then, blow out one breath for as long as you can. Have an adult partner time how many seconds your breath increases the squirt. Next, do jumping jacks or jump rope for two minutes. Then, repeat the test. Can you blow for more time or less time? To measure the results of this test another way, blow into a balloon. Use a measuring tape to see how full you are able to inflate it.

Then after exercising, inflate and
measure another balloon.

#3 You may have thought of other ideas,
but here's one that will work: Use
an eyedropper. Before dropping it
into the bottle, squeeze the rubber
bulb while the tip is in water to
get some water inside the tube. The
remaining air inside the eyedropper
will act like the air bubble in the
food packet.

#4 Hold the blow dryer with the nozzle
aimed straight up. Switch it on
"high." Then release the Ping-Pong
ball into the jet of air. The ball
will be suspended in the column
of fast-flowing air surrounded by
slower-moving air. NOTE: The heat
from the blow dryer will also heat
up the ball, so don't continue the
test for more than a couple of
minutes at a time.

#5 Like a bird's tail, a kite's tail
helps to create a smoother airflow

over the surface of the kite.
Your experiment should include
test flights during identical wind
conditions with a kite that has the
following:
1. No tail
2. A 4-inch-wide, 3-foot-long tail
(10-centimeter-wide, 0.9-meter-
long tail)
3. A 4-inch-wide, 6-foot-long tail
(10-centimeter-wide, 1.8-meter-
long tail).

You'll find that a tail makes it
easier to control the kite's flight.

#6 A leaf will continue to give off
water even after it's separated from
a plant. But since it no longer has
a fresh water supply, it will curl
and dry. To prevent water from
escaping, smear the leaf with a thin
coat of petroleum jelly. To see the
difference, compare two identical
leaves—one coated and one uncoated.

DARE YOURSELF!

Congratulations! You've successfully met the dares presented in this book. You're not finished, though. Now, science dares you to use what you've discovered about air: that it takes up space and exerts pressure, that air flow can be controlled to produce lift, and that moving air has force that can be used to do work. So create your own challenges. Then, brainstorm and plan experiments. Check with an adult partner to be sure what you want to try is safe to test. And let science help you meet all the dares you can dream up!

SCIENCE WORDS

AIR PRESSURE The force exerted on any surface by the total weight of all of the air against it.

COMPRESSED AIR Air that is under pressure.

EVAPORATION The process of a liquid changing to a gas.

LIFT The combination of forces that cause an object to rise into the air.

MOLECULE The smallest possible unit of something that can exist and have all of its characteristics.

SOUND Vibrations traveling through air, water, or a solid that can be detected by the ear, causing messages to be sent to the brain for analysis.

VIBRATION Any movement that follows the same path again and again.

WIND Air moving fast enough to be noticed. Wind is produced by warm air rising and cooler air flowing in to replace it.